CW00422427

Letts

Phonics Success

Age 5-6

Phonics

Louis Fidge
and
Christine
Moorcroft

**Practice
workbook**

Contents

Contents

Introduction

What is phonics?

Phonics is the relationship between sounds (phonemes) and letters or groups of letters (graphemes). Learning phonics involves listening to sounds, recognising sounds and discriminating between sounds as well as learning how sounds are represented by letters.

Phonics Practice Workbook is based on current practice in schools and presents letters and sounds in ways that should be familiar to children from their school work. This book will support parents and carers in helping children to learn to read and spell and to improve their reading and spelling using phonics.

Phonics for children (ages 5 to 6)

Literacy includes reading and writing, and phonics is important in both of these areas. This book builds on your child's previous learning (see *Phonics Practice Workbook Age 4–5*). It introduces a number of new sounds, and the letters that can represent the sounds, including different ways of spelling sounds they have already learned.

In addition to learning phonics, children should have opportunities to:
* read and enjoy stories, poems, rhymes and jingles
* read non-fiction texts, including signs, labels, captions, notes and so on.

This book helps children to learn the relationship between sounds and letters. They will learn:
* alphabetical order and the use of upper- and lower-case letters
* vowel sounds that are spelled using more than one letter
* different ways of spelling the same sounds
* different sounds represented by the same letters
* unusual spellings of vowel sounds, for example: 'or' for the 'ur' sound in words like 'worm', 'word' and 'work'
* unusual spellings of consonant sounds, for example: 'ph' for the 'f' sound; 'silent' letters, such as 'k' in 'knee', 'b' in 'comb', 't' in 'listen'.

How this book is organised

Letters of the alphabet (p. 6–11) further develops your child's understanding of upper- and lower-case letters, and alphabetical order.

Vowel digraphs introduces vowel sounds spelled with two letters: ay, ou, oy, ir, ea, aw, ew, oe, au, ie, ey for the 'ay' sound, and ey for the 'ee' sound.

Split digraphs features words with long vowel sounds (such as the 'i' in 'kite') that are spelled with two letters separated by a consonant (e.g. i–e in 'kite', a–e in bake).

Alternative vowel pronunciations introduces different ways of pronouncing vowels that have already been introduced. For example, the letter 'i' has been introduced for the 'i' sound in 'tip', 'bit' and so on, but it can also be pronounced in the same way as 'igh' in 'high' in words such as 'tiny', 'Ipod', 'mild'.

Alternative spellings for vowel sounds introduces different ways of spelling vowel sounds such as the 'or' sound in 'for'. This sound can also be spelled 'ore', 'oor' or 'our'.

Alternative spellings for consonant phonemes introduces different and more unusual ways of spelling the consonant sounds 'w' (wh), 'f' (ph), 'ch' (tch and tu) and 'j' (dge).

Alternative consonant pronunciations introduces less common ways of pronouncing consonants 'ch' (as 'k' in Christmas and as 'sh' in chef). Other unusual consonants introduced are 'ci' and 'ti' for 'sh' (as in 'special' and 'mention'), 's' for 'z' (as in 'please'), other 'c' and 'g' sounds and the 'zh' sound represented by 's' in words such as 'treasure'.

Silent letters features 'g', 'k', 'w', 'b' and 't' in words such as 'gnaw', 'knee', 'dumb' and 'listen'.

What have I learned?
This section provides activities to help you and your child assess what has been learned. It helps you to determine what further practice your child needs. Consult your child's teacher if you have any concerns.

Animal alphabet

Letters a–m

Say the name of each animal.
Write the letters for the first sound.
Write the first letter in the box.

 a<u></u>nt

 _at

 _at

 _og

 _lephant

 _rog

 _oat

 _orse

 _guana

 _aguar

 _angaroo

 _ion

 _ouse

Parent's tip

Ask your child to name the animal in each picture. Give help where necessary (especially for the more unusual animals, such as iguana). Then ask him/her to name the animal in the first picture. Ask your child to say the sound the word begins with and then to name the letter and write it in the box.

Animal alphabet

Letters n–z

Say the name of each animal.
Write the letters for the first sound.
Write the first letter in the box.

 <u>n</u>ewt

 _strich

 _anda

 _uail

 _abbit

 _nake

 _ortoise

 _mbrella bird

 _ulture

 _olf

 _-ray fish

 _ak

 _ebra

Parent's tip

Ask your child to name the animal in each picture. Give help where necessary (especially for the more unusual animals, such as vulture). Ask your child to say the sound the word begins with and then to name the letter and write it in the box. N.B. quail begins with the sound spelled qu although the first letter is q so your child should write qu.

7

Alphabetical order

Rocket alphabet

Take the rocket to each star in order.

Dot-to-dot alphabet

Join up the dots in alphabetical order to make a picture.

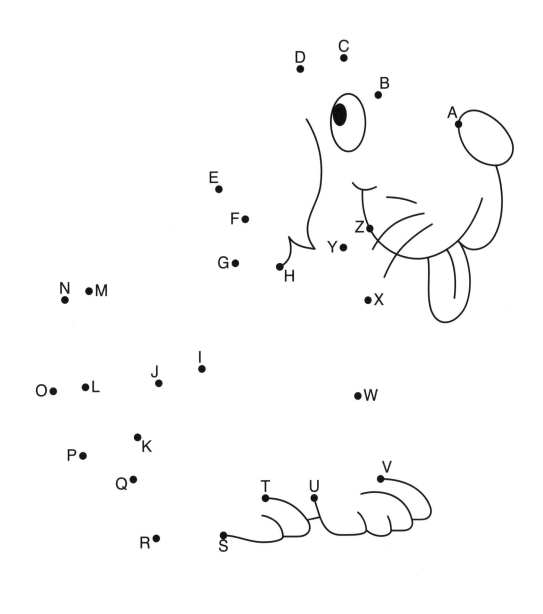

Parent's tip

Ask your child to find the first letter of the alphabet and say its name. Ask 'What comes next?' Ask questions such as: 'Which letter comes after h?', 'What comes after t?' and so on. After your child has completed the page ask: 'Which letter comes before b?', What comes before h?' and so on.

Upper- and lower-case letters

Words with ay

Read the rhyme

Circle **ay** in the rhyme.

I say, I say! Let's play today.

Hop away! Skip away!

May I play today?

Make the words

Make some words. Write the words. Read the words.

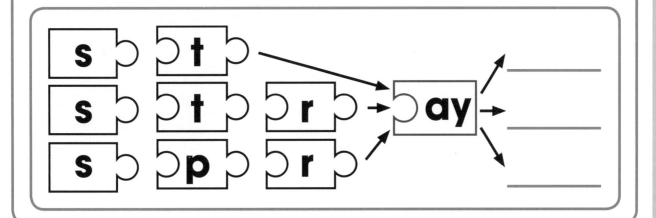

Parent's tip

Before beginning this page you could encourage your child to have fun making up rhymes. For example: 'Go away to Bombay', 'Don't play on the motorway', 'Stay on the pathway', 'I'll play with the spray', 'May has a tray of clay', 'Play with Jay', 'There's some hay in the bay'.

Words with ou

Read the rhyme

Circle **ou** in the rhyme.

The roundabout goes round and round.

We bound around for a pound.

We shout and shout.

On the roundabout.

Match the words

Read the words.
Match pairs of rhyming words.

Write the words.
Colour **ou** in the words.

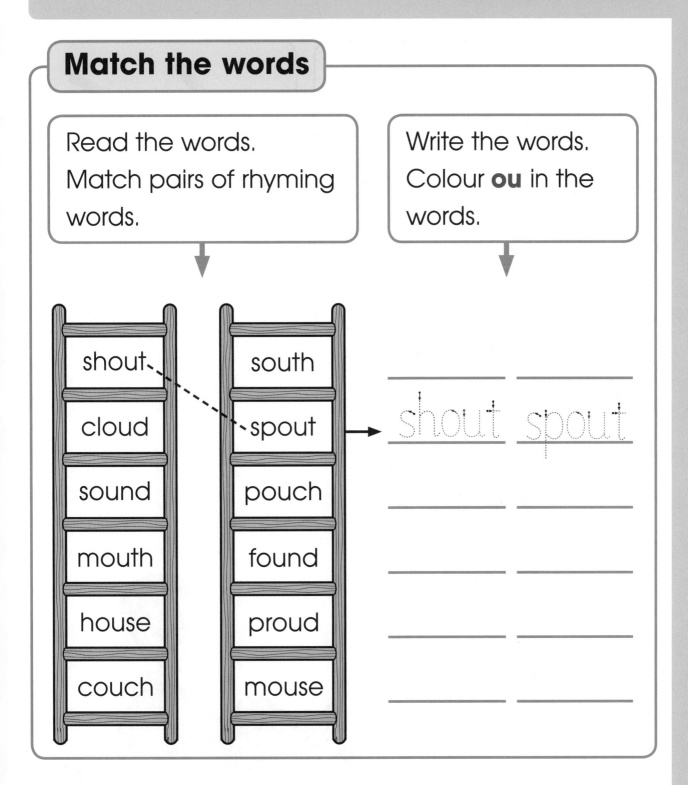

shout	south
cloud	spout
sound	pouch
mouth	found
house	proud
couch	mouse

shout   spout

Parent's tip

Read 'shout' and 'spout' aloud (emphasising the 'out' sounds). Ask your child what he/she notices about the sounds at the ends of the words. Point out the line that joins them 'because they rhyme'. Say the next word in the left-hand ladder ('cloud'), emphasising 'oud'. Tell your child that there is a rhyming word in the other ladder. Read the words in the right-hand ladder. Ask which word rhymes with 'cloud'.

Words with oy

Read the rhyme

Circle **oy** in the rhyme.

Joy is a girl. Roy is a boy.

They fell out over a toy.

"Let's enjoy it, not destroy it,

Don't annoy me," said Joy to Roy.

Words with oy

Make the words

Make some words. Read the words.

oy → b___   t___   enj___   ann___

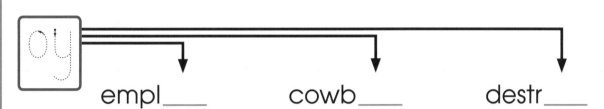

oy → empl___   cowb___   destr___

Write the words

Write the words in the grid.
Put one sound in each box.

Words with ir

Read the rhyme

Circle **ir** in the rhyme.

The first girl is thirsty.

The second girl's skirt is dirty.

The third girl, I'm glad to say,
is happy on her birthday!

Match the words

Read the words.
Match pairs of rhyming words.

Write the words.
Colour **ir** in the words.

sir
bird
first
skirt
girl

thirst
stir
third
twirl
shirt

sir   stir

Parent's tip

If necessary, explain that there are different ways of spelling the same sound. Write 'ir' and ask your child to say the sound 'ir' and give some examples of words he/she has learned that have 'ir' in them. Read 'sir' and 'stir' aloud (emphasising the 'ir' sounds). Ask your child what they notice about the sounds at the ends of the words. Point out the line that joins them 'because they rhyme'. Say the next word in the left-hand ladder ('bird'), emphasising 'ird'. Tell your child that there is a rhyming word in the other ladder. Read the words in the right-hand ladder. Ask which word rhymes with 'bird'.

Words with ea

b ea ch

beach

Read the rhyme

Circle **ea** in the rhyme.

      Play on the beach.

      Swim in the sea.

      Sit on a seat.

      Eat your tea!

Read the words

Read the words. Write the words.

ea → **t**	**s** → **ea** → **l**	**r** → **ea** → **d**
eat	_____	_____
t → **ea** → **ch**	**l** → **ea** → **p**	**b** → **ea** → **k**
_____	_____	_____

Write the words

Write the correct word under each picture.

_____

_____

_____

_____

_____

_____

Words with aw

Read the rhyme

Circle **aw** in the rhyme.

We hammer and saw.

We paint and draw.

I pad on my paws.

I grip with my claws.

Read the words

Read the words. Write the words.

s → aw	l → aw → n	d → r → aw
saw		
h → aw → k	th → aw	f → aw → n

Write the words

Write the correct word under each picture.

Words with ew

Read the rhyme

Circle **ew** in the rhyme.

I drew it!

I grew it!

I threw it!

Make the words

Make the words. Write the words. Read the words.

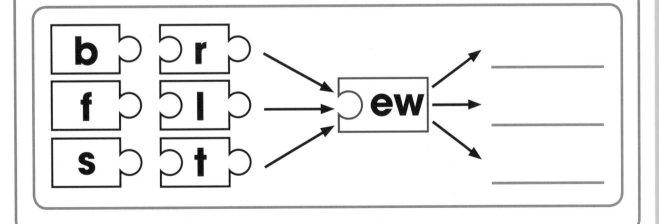

Parent's tip
If necessary, explain that there are different ways of spelling the same sound. Write 'ew' and ask your child to say the sound 'ew' and give some examples of words he/she has learned that have 'ew' in them. For example: chew, grew, flew, drew, threw.

Words with ue

Make the words

Make some words and names. Read the words.

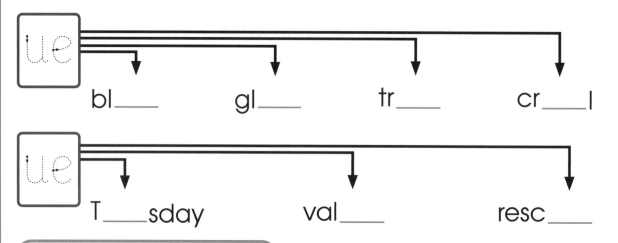

ue

bl____   gl____   tr____   cr____l

ue

T____sday   val____   resc____

Write the words

Write the words in the grid. Put one sound in each box.

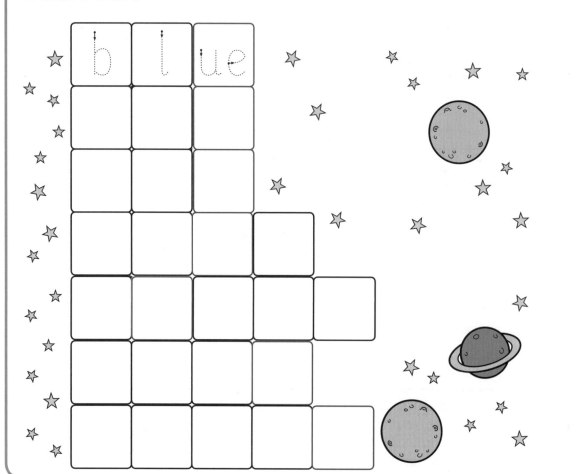

Make the words

Make some words and names. Read the words.

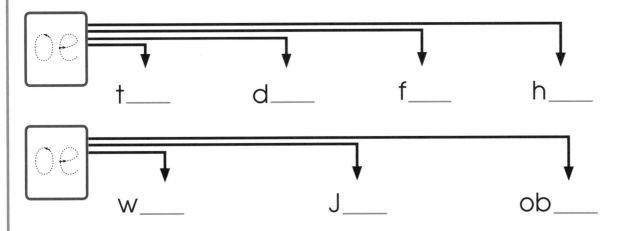

oe ⟶ t___ d___ f___ h___

oe ⟶ w___ J___ ob___

Write the words

Write the words in the grid. Put one sound in each box.

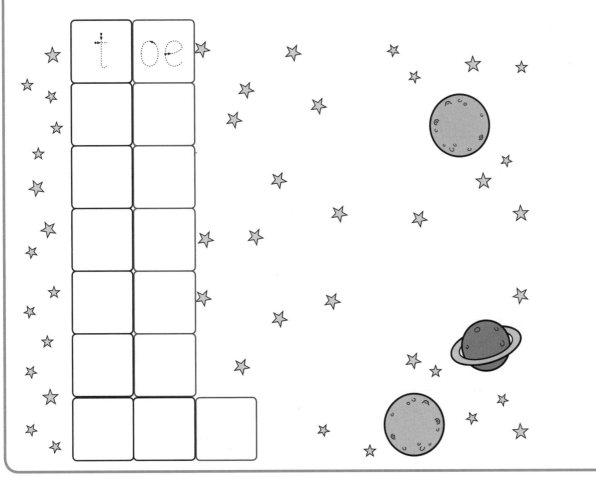

Words with au

Make the words

Make some words and names. Read the words.

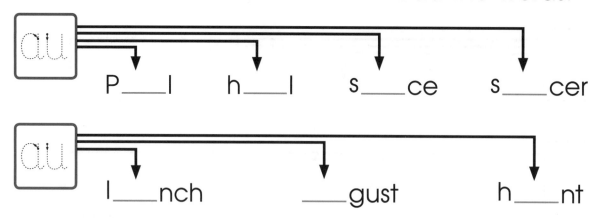

au → P___l   h___l   s___ce   s___cer

au → l___nch   ___gust   h___nt

Write the words

Write the words in the grid. Put one sound in each box.

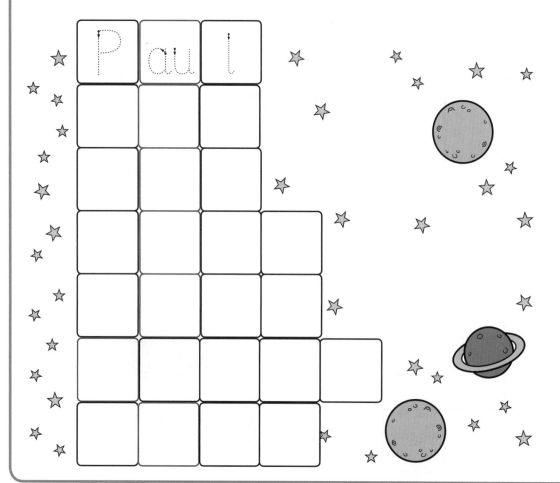

Make the words

Make some words with **ie**. Read the words.

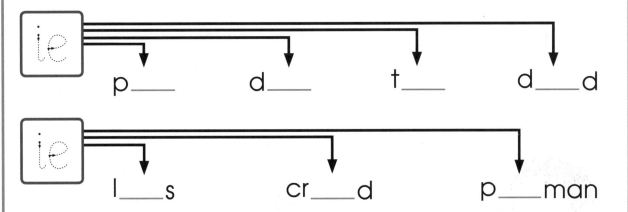

ie ———→ p___   d___   t___   d___d

ie ———→ l___s   cr___d   p___man

Write the words

Write the words in the grid. Put one sound in each box.

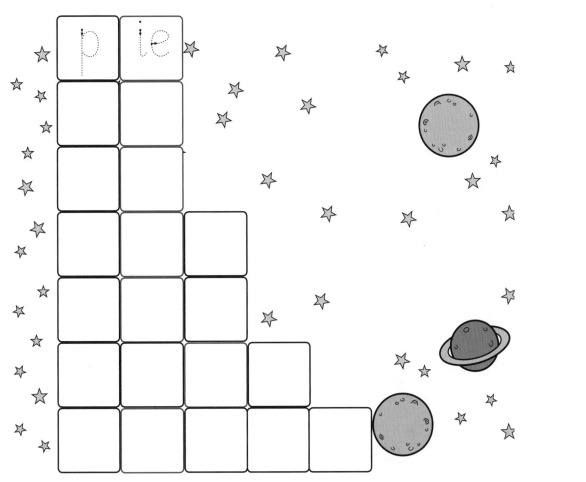

When ey says ay

Make some words

Make some words with **ey**. Read the words.

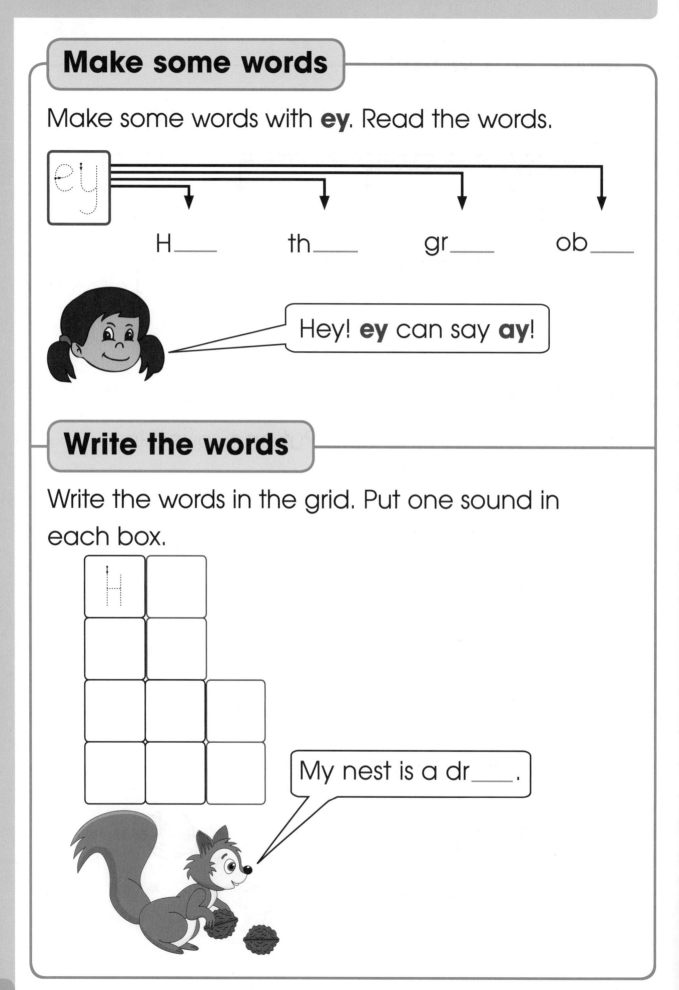

ey

H_____   th_____   gr_____   ob_____

Hey! **ey** can say **ay**!

Write the words

Write the words in the grid. Put one sound in each box.

My nest is a dr_____.

Make the words

Make the words with **ey**.

Read the words. Write the words.

| a | bb | | → _____

| j | o | ck | | → _____

| d | o | n | k | | → _____

| t | ur | k | | → _____

| ch | i | m | n | | → _____

Split digraph a-e

Read the story

Colour **a-e** in the story. Join **a-e**.

1 Wake up.

2 Make the bed.

3 Shake the mat.

4 Rake the leaves.

5 Bake a cake.

6 Take a nap!

Write the words

Write the **a͡-e͡** words.

 f a c e w

Match the words

Match up the rhyming words.

Write the words. Read the words.

made
gale
name
plate
lane
cave

sale
skate
spade
mane
save
tame

made _spade_

Split digraph i-e

Read the rhyme

Colour **i-e** in the rhyme. Join **i-e**.

Sail down the Nile,
And after a mile
You will see a crocodile
With a fine smile!

Write the words

Write the **î-ê** words.

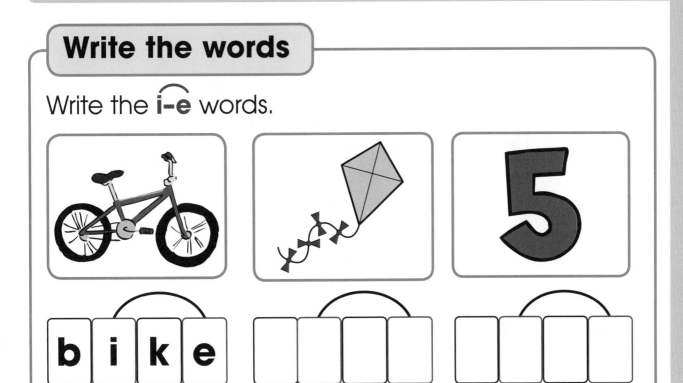

b	i	k	e

Match the words

Match up the rhyming words.

Write the words.
Read the words.

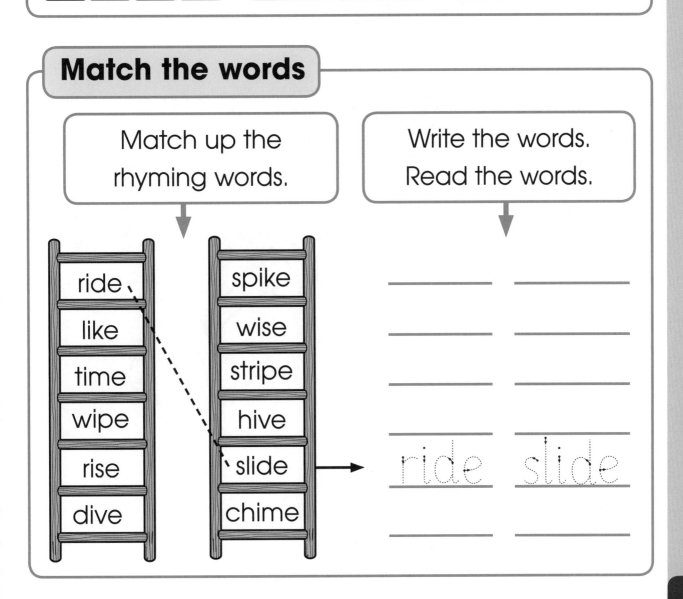

ride
like
time
wipe
rise
dive

spike
wise
stripe
hive
slide
chime

ride   slide

Split digraph o-e

Read the rhyme

Colour **o-e** in the rhyme. Join **o-e**.

Old King Cole
Fell down a hole.
He broke a bone
On a big stone.

Write the words

Write the **o-e** words.

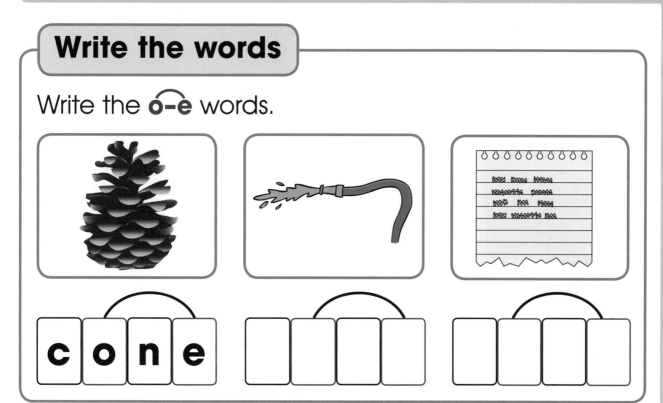

Match the words

Match up the rhyming words.

Write the words.
Read the words.

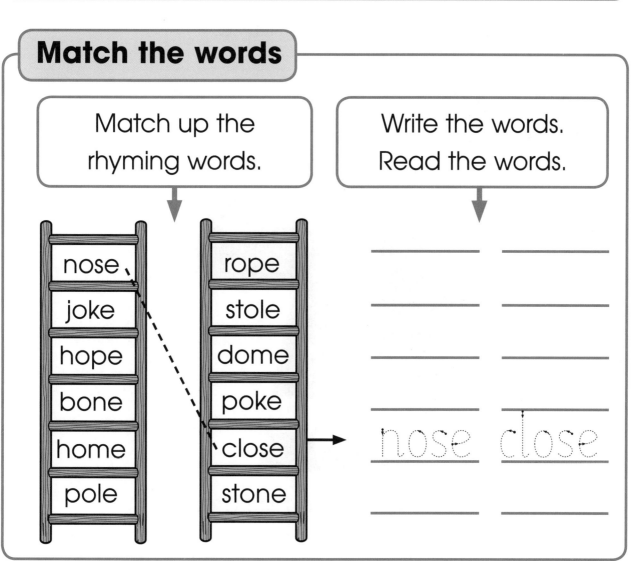

nose   close

Split digraph u͡-e

Read the rhyme

Colour **u-e** in the rhyme. Join **u͡-e**.

Duke Luke plays a tune on his flute.

Split digraph u-e

Write the words

Write the **u-e** words.

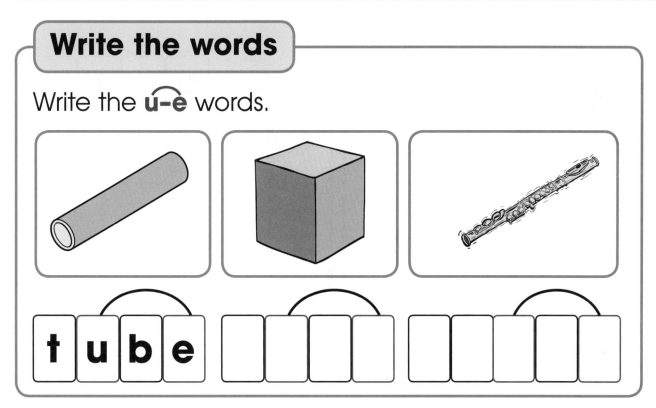

t | u | b | e

Match the words

Match up the rhyming words.

Write the words. Read the words.

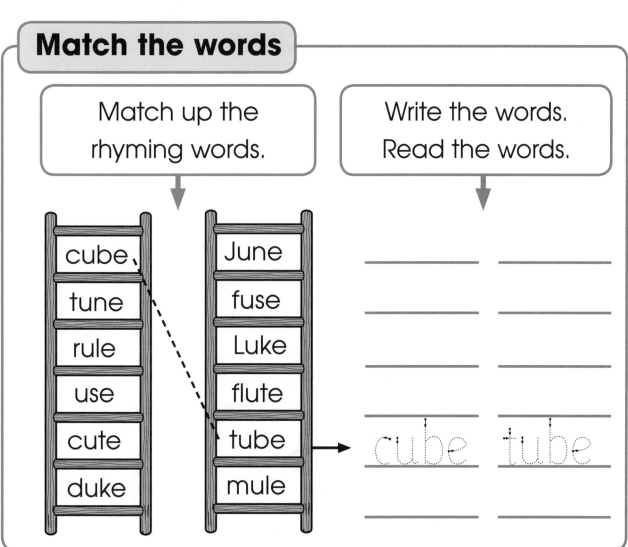

cube
tune
rule
use
cute
duke

June
fuse
Luke
flute
tube
mule

cube   tube

Split digraph e-e

My name is Eve.

My name is Pete.

Make the words

Make the words and names with **e-e**.
Read the words. Write the words.

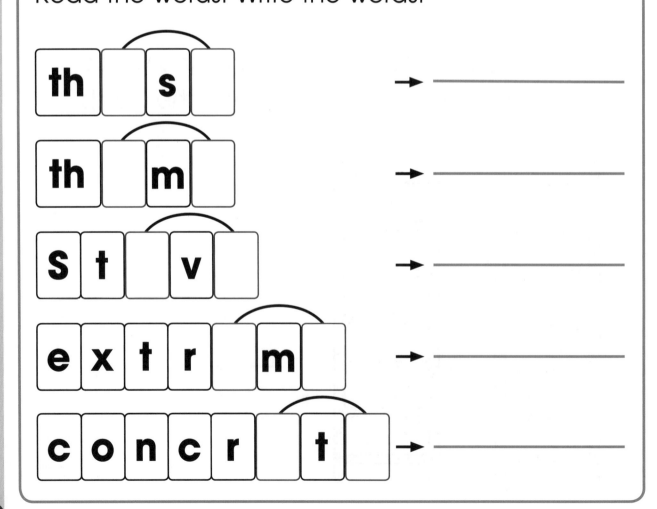

Complete the words

Complete the words with **i**. Read the words.
Write the words.

| f | i | n | d | | m | | n | d | | b | | n | d |

_____   _____   _____

Make the words

Make the words with **i**.
Read the words. Write the words.

| ch | | l | d | → _____

| w | | l | d | → _____

| p | | n | t | → _____

| k | | n | d | → _____

| b | e | h | | n | d | → _____

When a says ar

Write the word

Write the word for each picture. Read the words.

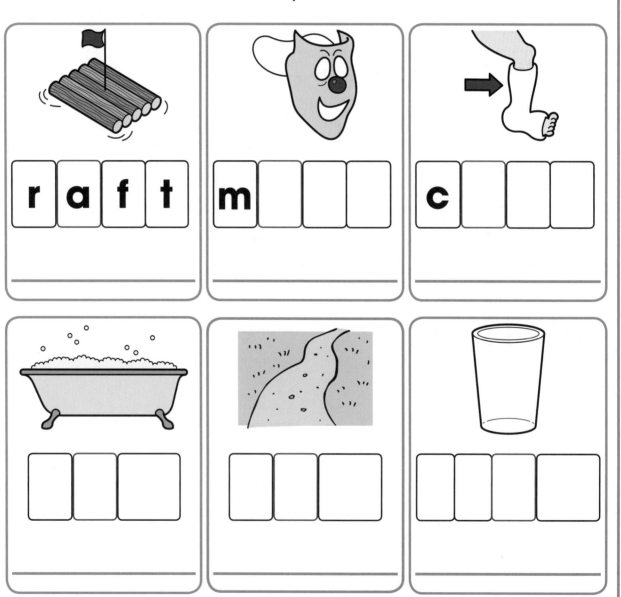

Parent's tip This page is not appropriate where the regional pronunciation is 'a' as in 'cat'.

Make the words

Make the words with **a**.

Read the words. Write the words.

| p | r | o | n | → _____

| p | r | i | l | → _____

b | | s | i | n | → _____

J | | s | o | n | → _____

| p | r | i | c | o | t | → _____

Parent's tip   Remind your child that names start with a capital letter.

A different u sound

b **u** **sh**

bush

Read the rhyme

Circle **u** in the rhyme.

Never pull or push

A bull in a bush.

For if you do,

It may push you, too!

Parent's tip This page is not appropriate where the regional pronunciation is 'u' as in 'cup'.

Choose the word

Choose the correct word for each picture.

full	pull

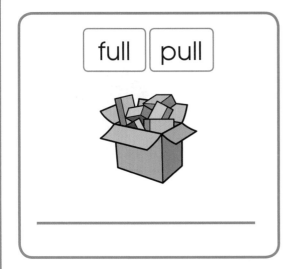

_____

pull	bull

_____

bush	push

_____

push	put

_____

bull	bush

_____

pull	push

_____

When o says u

Write the words

Write the word for each picture.
They all rhyme.

love   d ___

_____   _____   _____

Match the words

Match the rhyming words.	Write the words. Read the words.

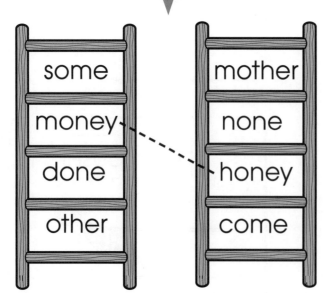

some   mother

money   none

done   honey

other   come

_____   _____

_____   _____

_____   _____

_____   _____

Write the name of a day
of the week with o.

_____

p | er | m

perm

f | er | n

fern

Make the words

Make the words with **er**.

Read the words. Write the words.

| j | | k | → | _____ |

| t | | m | → | _____ |

| k | | b | → | _____ |

| s | t | | n | → | _____ |

| p | | ch | → | _____ |

When ow says oh

snow

Read the rhyme

Circle **ow** in the rhyme.

I can row.

I can mow.

I can blow.

I can grow!

Parent's tip   Your child might know words in which 'ow' represents the 'ow' sound in 'cow'. Point out that 'ow' can be used for a different sound – in glow, show, grow, snow and many other words.

Swop the sound

Read the words.	Swap the first sound for:	Write the words. Read the words.
low	m	mow
tow	r	
crow	g	
blow	s	
glow	f	
grow	c	
follow	h	
borrow	s	
yellow	b	
pillow	w	
narrow	b	

When ie says ee

Write the words

Write the words with **ie**. Read the words.

| ch | ie | f | | th | ie | f | | b | r | ie | f |

_____ _____ _____

Make the words

Make the words with **ie**.
Read the words. Write the words.

| f | | l | d | → _____

| sh | | l | d | → _____

| p | r | | s | t | → _____

| sh | r | | k | → _____

| b | e | l | | f | → _____

j	e	ll	y

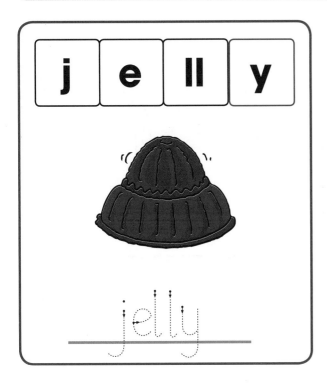

jelly

m	u	mm	y

mummy

Make the words

Make the words with **y**.

Read the words. Write the words.

| h | o | ll | |

→ _____

| l | a | z | |

→ _____

| h | a | pp | |

→ _____

| oi | l | |

→ _____

| e | v | er | |

→ _____

When ea says e

Read the rhyme

Circle **ea** in the rhyme.

The little bird is pecking for bread.

Bob, bob, bob goes its head.

It flaps its wings and shakes its feathers.

It visits my garden in all kinds of weather.

Swop the sound

Read the words.	Swap the first sound for:	Write the words.
head	d	dead
bread	d	
thread	s p	
feather	w	
leather	h	
ready	s t	
healthy	w	
death	b r	

Parent's tip Your child might know words in which 'ea' represents the 'ea' sound (like ee) in 'meat'. Point out that 'ea' can be used for a different sound – in dead, bread, head, deaf and many other words.

When y says igh

Read the rhyme

Circle **y** in the rhyme.

Why do you cry? Why do you cry?

Soon you'll be a butterfly.

And flutter by in the sky!

Make the words

Make the **y** words.

Read the words. Write the words.

m_____   sh_____   sl_____   sp_____

_my_   _____   _____   _____

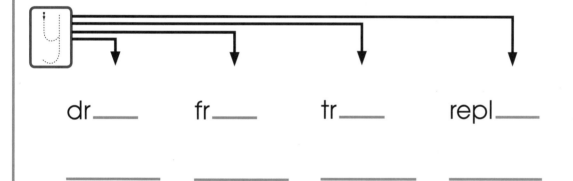

dr_____   fr_____   tr_____   repl_____

_____   _____   _____   _____

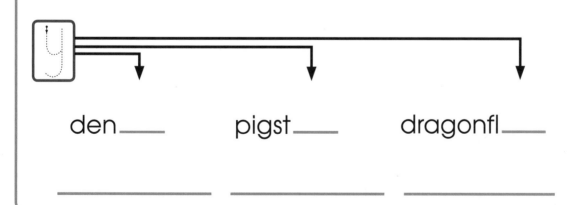

den_____   pigst_____   dragonfl_____

_____   _____   _____

Parent's tip Your child might know words in which 'y' represents the 'y' sound (like ee) in 'silly'. Point out that 'y' can be used for a different sound – in sky, my, by, try and many other words.

When or says ur

worm

world

Make the words

Make the words with **or**.

Read the words. Write the words.

| w | | d | → _____ |

| w | | k | → _____ |

| w | | th | → _____ |

| w | | s | t | → _____ |

| w | | sh | i | p | → _____ |

p	al	m

palm

al	m	o	n	d

almond

Make the words

Make the words with **al**.

Read the words. Write the words.

c		f

→ _____

h		f

→ _____

c		m

→ _____

l	i	p	b		m

→ _____

When ear says er

Read the rhyme

Circle **ear** in the rhyme.

Teddy bear, teddy bear,

Your coat has a tear.

Teddy bear, teddy bear,

What will you wear?

Make the words

Make some words.

Write the words.

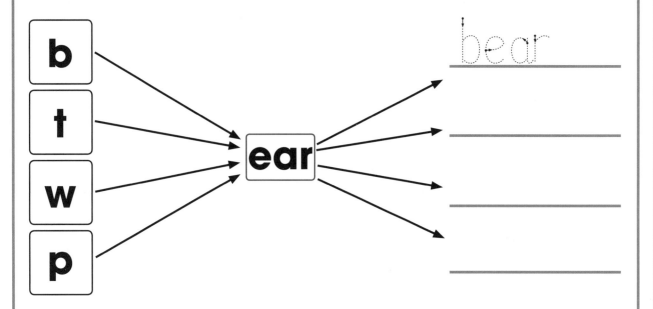

b		
t		
w	ear	
p		

bear

Use the words to fill in the crossword.

Down

1. A large wild animal
2. To dress in something

Across

3. A kind of fruit
4. To rip something

When are says air

Read the rhyme

Circle **are** in the rhyme.

Once I saw a rare hare.

"Stare at me if you dare," said the hare.

"I don't care!"

I have stares to spare.

Make the words

Make some words with **are**. Read the words.
Write the words.

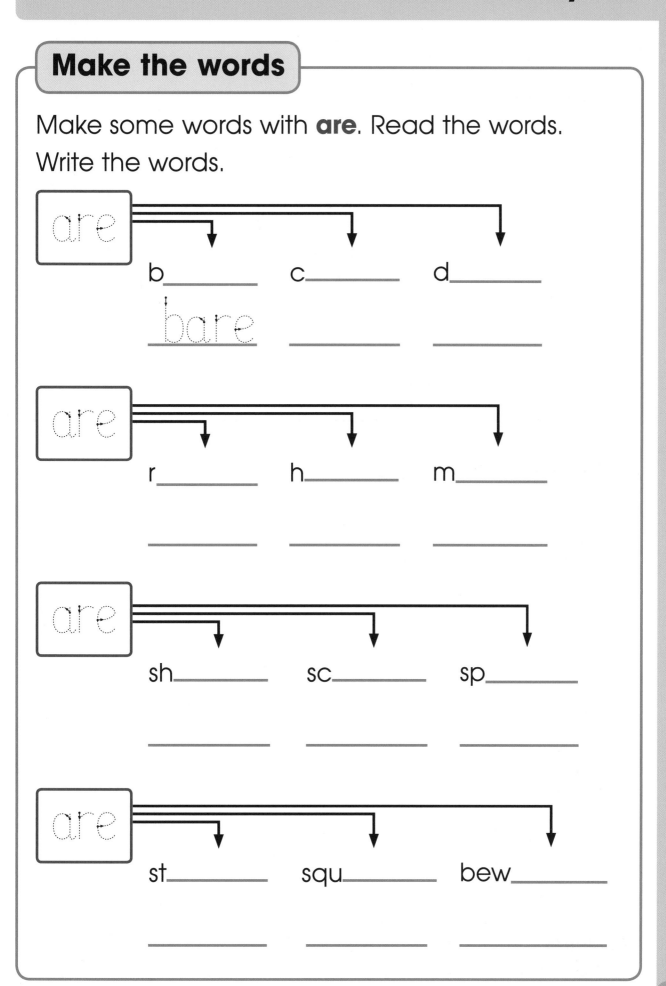

are → b_____   c_____   d_____

bare   _____   _____

are → r_____   h_____   m_____

_____   _____   _____

are → sh_____   sc_____   sp_____

_____   _____   _____

are → st_____   squ_____   bew_____

_____   _____   _____

Words with eer

deer

Make the words

Make the words with **eer**.

Read the words. Write the words.

j		→ _____
p		→ _____
sh		→ _____
s	t		→ _____

Parent's tip

Practise saying the 'eer' sound in 'deer' with your child. Explain that all the words have this sound and that even if your child hasn't seen or heard these words before he/she can read them by sounding the letters.

Sort the words

Read the words.

Sort the words into sets.

ear words	**eer** words

Words with oor

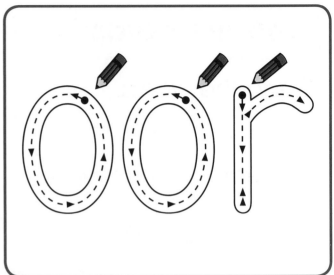

Make the words

Make the words with **oor**.

Read the words. Write the words.

| d | | → _____ |

| m | | → _____ |

| p | | → _____ |

| f | l | | → _____ |

| t | a | n | d | | i | → _____ |

Join the words

Make words from door + another word.

Write the words.

doormat

_____man

_____way

_____bell

_____step

trap_____

Parent's tip

Point out to your child that they have learned different ways of spelling the sound 'or'. Revisit page 64 and ask yours child to read the word at the top of the page. Ask which letters spell the sound 'or'.

Tell your child that the words on this page have 'oor' in them. When your child has written the words, ask him/her to read them.

Words with ore

Read the rhyme

Circle **ore** in the rhyme.

Snore! Snore! Snore!
I can't stand any more.
I've told Dad before
That his snore is a bore!

Make the words

Make some words with **ore**. Read the words.

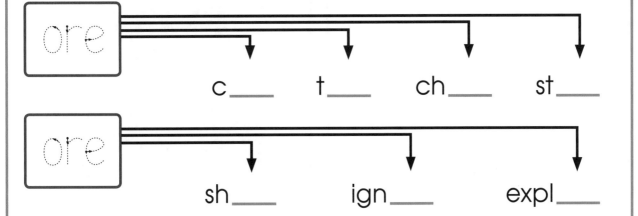

c____   t___   ch____   st____

sh____   ign____   expl____

Write the words

Write the words in the grid. Put one sound in each box.

Words with our

p | our

pour

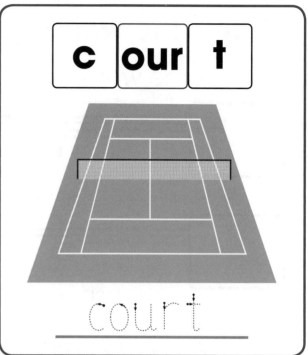

c | our | t

court

Make the words

Make the words with **our**.
Read the words. Write the words.

y ☐ → _____

f ☐ → _____

f ☐ th → _____

f ☐ t ee n → _____

c ☐ t y ar d → _____

d | augh | t | er

daughter

Make the words

Make the words with **augh**.

Read the words. Write the words.

| d | | t | er | → _____ |

| n | | t | y | → _____ |

| c | | t | | → _____ |

| t | | t | | → _____ |

| s | l | | t | er | → _____ |

Words with al

w	al	k

walk

t	al	k

talk

Make the words

Make the words with **al**.

Read the words. Write the words.

ch		k

→ _____

s	t		k

→ _____

w		k	er

→ _____

b	ea	n	s	t		k

→ _____

s	i	d	e	w		k

→ _____

Make the words

Make the words with **all**.

Read the words. Write the words.

Words with wh

Read the words

Read the words that begin **wh**. Circle **wh** in the words.

Write two questions:

When _____

Why _____

Words with wh

Make the words

Make some words with **wh**. Write the words.
Read the words.

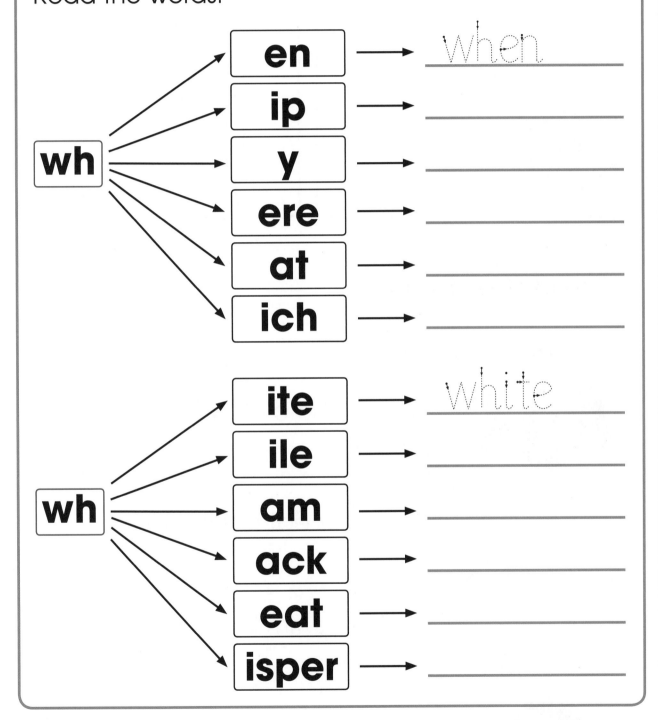

wh	**en**	when
	ip	
	y	
	ere	
	at	
	ich	

wh	**ite**	white
	ile	
	am	
	ack	
	eat	
	isper	

Parent's tip Ask your child which letter to use for the sound 'w' (say the sound, not the letter name). He/she should know that the letter is 'w'. Then ask if he/she knows how to spell 'when'. If so, point out the letters 'wh'. Tell him/her that there are a few words that have 'wh' for the 'w' sound.

Words with ph

Read the rhyme

Circle **ph** in the rhyme.

We call the alphabet the ABC.

Elephants eat leaves from a tree.

Dolphins swim in the deep blue sea.

All my friends phone me!

Make the words

Make some words with **ph**. Read the words.
Write the words.

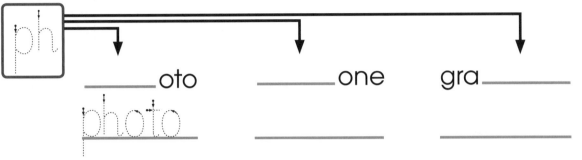

____oto   ____one   gra____

photo   _____   _____

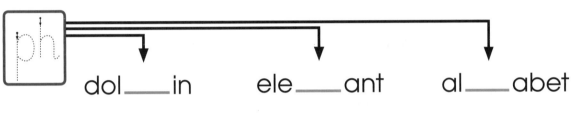

dol____in   ele____ant   al____abet

_____   _____

Write the words

Write the correct word under each picture.

____

____

____

____

____

____

Words with tch

Read the rhyme

Circle **tch** in the rhyme.

We're all at the match.

See that catch!

Bowling down the pitch.

Oh, no! He's in the ditch!

Make the words

Make some words with **tch**. Read the words.

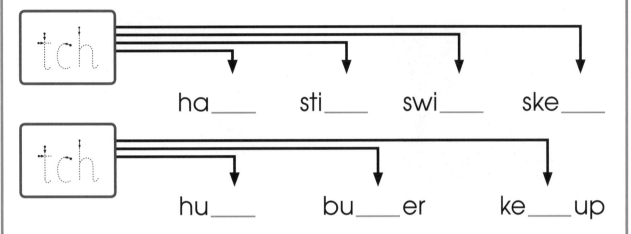

tch ⟶ ha____ sti____ swi____ ske____

tch ⟶ hu____ bu____er ke____up

Write the words

Write the words in the grid. Put one sound in each box.

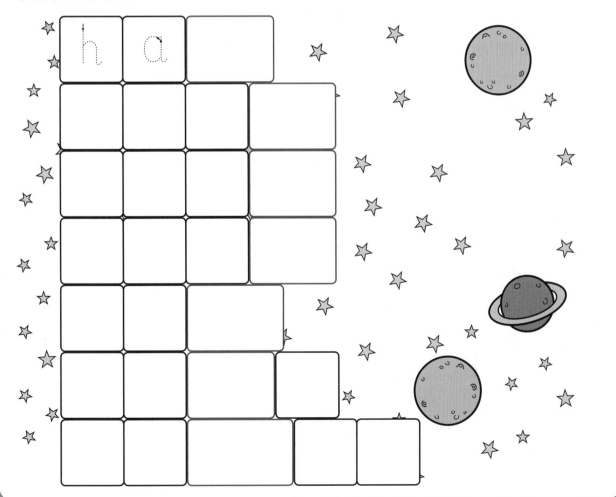

h | a |

Words with dge

j	u	dge

judge

b	r	i	dge

bridge

Make the words

Make the words with **dge**.

Read the words. Write the words.

d	o	

→ _____

h	e	

→ _____

f	u	

→ _____

b	a	

→ _____

b	a		er

→ _____

Make the words

Make the words with **tu**.

Read the words. Write the words.

n	a		re	→ _____
c	a	p		re	→ _____
f	u		re	→ _____
m	i	x		re	→ _____
p	u	n	c		re	→ _____

When ch says k

Read the rhyme

Circle **ch** in the rhyme.

One day at home I baked a cake,
But it gave me a stomach ache!
I had to go to the chemist shop
For something to make my stomach ache stop!

Make the words

Complete each word with **ch**.
Read the words.

e____o	s____ool	an____or
____oir	stoma____	____emist

Write the words

Write the correct word under each picture.

When g says j

germ

page

Read the rhyme

Circle **g** that says j in the rhyme.

Gina and Gerry live on a barge.

But the barge isn't large.

So it's not at all strange.

That they fancy a change.

Write the words

Write the word for each picture. Read the words.

an_____

g_____

ma_____

dan_____

hin_____

sta_____

Write the words with **g** that says j.
Circle **g** in the words.

A room in a house   loun_____

The front of your hair   frin_____

A boy's name   Ro_____

When s says z

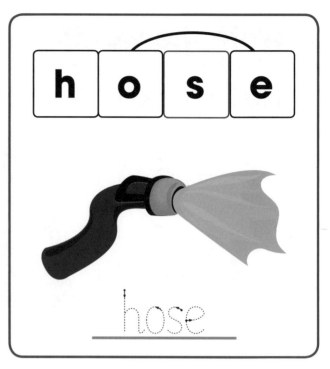

Read the rhyme

Circle **s** in the rhyme.

The rose grows if I use the hose.

My nose knows when the rose grows!

I suppose the rose knows when I use the hose.

Write the words

Read the clues.
Write the words with **s** that says z.
Read the words.

A food made from milk. ch_____

Not hard to do. ea_____

A loud sound. n_____

A girl's shirt. blou_____

A polite word. plea_____

To take your pick. ch_____

Parent's tip
Write the letter 's' and ask what sound it says. Your child should know the 's' sound as in 'see', 'sit', etc. Tell him/her that in some words 's' says the same sound as 'z'. Write and say some examples. For example: use, rise, rose, nose.

When c says s

cell

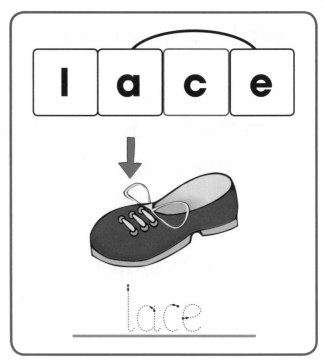

lace

Read the rhyme

Circle **c** that says s in the rhyme.

Cilla went to the cinema
On an icy day in December.
She had no lock for her bicycle
So she tied it to an icicle.

Write the words

Read the clues.
Write the words with **c** that says s.
Read the words.

More than one mouse.   mi_____

This is a smiley   f_____.

A food that goes
with curry.   r_____

White stuff spread on
a cake.   i_____

You roll these to get
a score.   d_____

You run fast in a   r_____.

When ci says sh

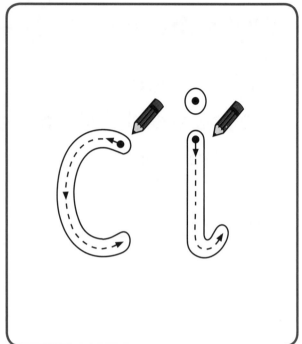

Make the words

Make the words with **ci** that says sh. Write the words. Read the words.

| o | p | t | i | | a | n | → _____

| s | o | | a | l | → _____

| s | p | e | | a | l | → _____

| m | u | s | i | | a | n | → _____

| t | e | l | e | v | i | si | o | n |

television

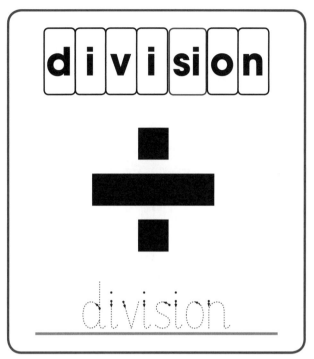

| d | i | v | i | si | o | n |

division

Read the rhyme

Circle **s** that says zh in the rhyme.

I look for treasure.

It's a pleasure

To measure the treasure.

89

When gn says n

sign

gnome

Make the words

Make the words with **gn** that says n.
Read the sentences.

A ☐ **a** **t** is an insect that bites.

A dog will ☐ **aw** a bone.

If it's angry it might ☐ **a** **sh** its teeth.

kn	i	t

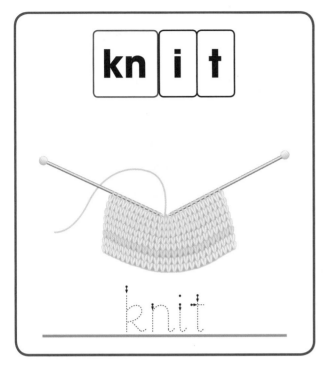

knit

kn	i	ck	er	s

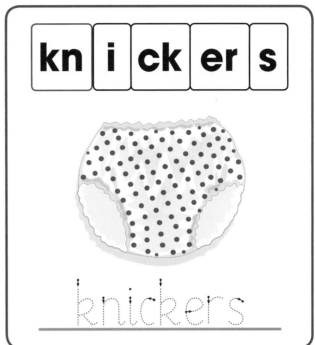

knickers

Make the words

Make the words with **kn** that says n.

Read the rhyme.

This is the [ ] **igh** **t** that lost his [ ] **i** **f** **e** .

He [ ] **o** **ck** **s** on the door

Where's my knife?

And [ ] **ee** **l** **s** on the floor.

When wr says r

wren

write

Make the words

Make the words with **wr** that says r.
Read the rhyme.

I [ ] **o** **t** **e** a word.

It wasn't long.

But the [ ] **i** **t** **i** **ng** was [ ] **o** **ng**.

What a [ ] **e** **ck** of a word

I [ ] **o** **t** **e**.

When mb says m

Make the words

Make the words with **mb** that says m.

Write the words. Read the words.

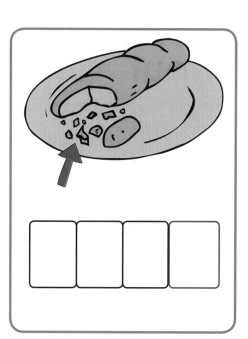

What have I learned?

Note to parents	Present the tests one at a time. Explain that they will show your child what he/she has learned. Use encouraging words such as 'See if you can read the words in this test by yourself'. Tell your child that there will be some words he/she might never have heard before but that they can be sounded using what your child knows about letters and sounds. Explain to your child what to do. For correct answers, use words such as 'Well done', 'You did well.' If incorrect, praise your child for having a try: 'It doesn't matter if you get things wrong. That's how we know what you need to practise.'

Read the words and names.

Test 1

tray	loud
today	Roy
snout	deploy

Test 2

dirt	reach
birch	law
beak	pawn

Test 3

new	Tuesday
drew	Joe
fuel	oboe

Test 4

haul	race
tied	slate
turkey	hike

Read the words and names.

Test 5

poke	tiny
jawbone	limb
tune	acorn

Test 6

monkey	dead
fern	fly
slow	worth

Test 7

calm	spare
heard	cheer
Clare	floor

Test 8

doorway	pour
core	naughty
before	always

Test 9

call	while
install	photo
when	optician

Test 10

match	badge
itch	Phil
fetch	picture

What have I learned?

Read the words and names.

Test 11

kneel	action
chef	badger
obey	echo

Test 12

vision	magic
facial	gnome
gym	adventure

Test 13

wreck	playtime
listen	fairground
fracture	inside

Test 14

sound	borrow
auburn	Stephen
brief	these